Praise for The Mindful Doodle Book

"This book invites readers to a delightful new way to wake up to our lives. No matter what you're doing – digesting, doubting, deep thinking, or divorcing – there's a doodle for it. The author knows how to bring out the artist in each of us as she teaches us to hold our experience and ourselves in loving awareness. So go ahead, doodle it!"

Christopher Germer, PhD, author of *The Mindful Path to Self-Compassion*
Faculty, Harvard Medical School

"Everyone needs to play--adults and children alike! Play is at the cutting-edge of growth and creativity. *The Mindful Doodle Book* is a fun-filled journey towards self-expression and self-discovery. This bottom-up approach frees the hand in order to focus the mind and open the heart."

-Terry Marks-Tarlow, PhD, author of *Clinical Intuition in Psychotherapy, Awakening Clinical Intuition*, and the upcoming *Colors of Mindfulness*

"With *The Mindful Doodle Book*, Patricia Isis has created a perfect bridge for the ordinary person into the realm of mindfulness. By taking the universal practice of doodling and placing it in a thoughtful context of meaning and kindness, anyone can achieve a level of emotional understanding and relief from the stress and challenge of everyday life. This book can serve as a daily practice for individuals, a useful adjunct to therapy or coaching and an independent means of learning to deal productively with just about anything that comes up. A ten minute Mindful Doodle session before school, a doctor's appointment, a competition or business meeting might be the most cost-effective health intervention anyone could make!"

-Pat B. Allen, PhD, ATR, author of *Art Is a Way of Knowing* and *Art Is a Spiritual Path*

"Thank-you for *The Mindful Doodle Book*! Finally, a resource for practitioners in mental health which offers simple drawing prompts to supplement therapeutic communication. The Mindful Doodle Book is an interactive hands-on approach intended for diverse clients of various ages and backgrounds. Author, Patricia Isis, PhD, ATR-BC, is a Board Certified Art Therapist, Licensed Mental Health Counselor and a Trained Instructor in Mindful Self-Compassion. Combining both her practices in Art Therapy and Mindfulness, Dr. Isis' innovative ideas are now collected and elaborated in this unique guide. All the exercises have no right or wrong result, and require minimal equipment and even less artistic know-how. The author makes a distinction between the administration of the drawing exercises by a certified art therapist and by professionals with no art therapy education. Directions for referrals to professional art therapists are included. Professionals of all backgrounds will find this book a valuable addition to their practice."

-Janet Bush,EDS, ATR-BC, author of *The Handbook of School Art Therapy: Introducing Art Therapy into a Public School System*

"All children love to spontaneously draw, but we grow older, we become more self-conscious and judgmental. This delightful book uses artful doodling to help us and our clients rekindle our ability to be mindfully present in the moment, engage our senses, and identify and embrace our emotions more fully."

--Richard Sears, PsyD, PhD, ABPP, author of *Mindfulness: Living through Challenges and Enriching Your Life in this Moment*

The MINDFUL Doodle BOOK

75 Creative Exercises to Help You Live in the Moment

Patricia Isis, Ph.D. ATR-BC, LMHC, ATCS

Published by
PESI Publishing & Media
PESI, INC
3839 White Avenue
Eau Claire, WI 54703

Cover: Al Postlewaite
Layout: Bookmasters & Al Postlewaite
ISBN: 9781683730118
All Rights Reserved.
Printed in the United States of America

PESI
Publishing
& Media
www.pesipublishing.com

About the Author

Patricia Isis, Ph.D. ATR-BC, LMHC, ATCS

Board Certified Registered Art Therapist, Licensed Mental Health Counselor
Art Therapist Certified Supervisor, Licensed Mental Health Counselor Supervisor

Dr. Isis completed her Ph.D. in the expressive therapies with an emphasis on art therapy in 2003 from the Union Institute and University in Cincinnati, Ohio. In 1980, Dr. Isis attained her Master's degree in Expressive Therapies with an emphasis on Art Therapy from Lesley University in Cambridge, Massachusetts. Maintaining a mindfulness meditation practice for many years, Dr. Isis received training in MBSR with Jon Kabat-Zinn and Saki Santorelli in June of 2000. Since that time, she has conducted Mindfulness-based stress reduction (MBSR) classes for Baptist Health at South Miami Hospital. Since January 2013, Dr. Isis has been offering MBSR and mindfulness trainings in her South Miami office.

Dr. Isis has been practicing art psychotherapy in South Florida for over 35 years. She has worked in schools, hospitals, day treatment programs, substance abuse, eating disorder treatment centers and residential settings. Currently, she provides individual, couples, family and group art therapy/counseling and mindfulness trainings privately and offers full time clinical services in the public schools. Dr. Isis is a trained Mindful Self-Compassion Teacher under the direction of Drs. Christopher Germer and Kristin Neff who are the creators of the evidenced-based 8 week program.

Dr. Isis is a popular presenter/instructor for courses, workshops and trainings locally, nationally, and internationally. More information is available on her website at www.MiamiArtTherapy.com

Acknowledgements

This book is dedicated to the magic of mindfulness and art therapy, a magnificent blend of presence and healing. I am sitting here filled with tremendous appreciation and gratitude for all the generous people who supported the birth of this book.

Beginning with my art teacher, Mr. Adams who inspired me from the age of 4-11 to use art as a healing force in my life. Professors at Lesley College in the Expressive Therapies program and Union Institute and University. Mindfulness-based Stress Reduction training with Dr. Jon Kabat-Zinn, and Saki Santorelli,. More recently, Mindful Self- Compassion Teacher Training with Dr. Christopher Germer, Dr. Kristin Neff, Steve Hickman and Michelle Becker.

I thank my precious art therapy tribal/family members, Janet Bush, Pat Allen, Barbara Fish, Gussie Klorer, David Gussak, Marcia Rosal, Christianne Strang and Terri Halperin-Eaton who looked over the material and offered many pearls of wisdom.

More gratitude as well to Karsyn Morse at PESI for ongoing enthusiasm as the book unfolded. I also thank my loving family, friends, co-workers, teachers, mentors, students, and clients.

I hold endless appreciation to Julianne, my curious and adventurous daughter who is an amazing model of presence and purpose.

Table of Contents

Welcome to Mindful Doodling

Close your eyes.
Fall in Love.
Stay there.
-Rumi

Being a helping professional is incredibly rewarding and demanding simultaneously. However, after more than 35 years of mindfulness meditation and art therapy practice, I continue to have a love affair with my work. Much of this experience, I credit to the ongoing cultivation of moment to moment non-judgmental awareness or mindfulness combined with artmaking opportunities and explorations for my clients and myself.

Since you picked up this book, I suspect that you are interested in developing a mindfulness-based doodle practice for yourself and your clients as well.

Consider the following inquiries:

What is your relationship to mindfulness in your life?
Do you currently use art in your work?
Do you make your own art in response to your clinical experiences?
Do you understand the difference between art therapy and therapeutic art making?

No matter what your answers are to these questions, this book will offer you many options for mindfulness-based doodling inside and outside your clinical work and ways to utilize these tools ethically. Whether you are familiar with mindfulness practices or therapeutic artmaking, both are available to you here through mindful doodling.

Mindfulness enhances balance, clarity, and wellness through acceptance of momentary awareness (Kabat-Zinn, 1990). Doodling, the most common and ignored art form for intuitive expression has been around since the oldest cave paintings. Mindfulness and doodling together serve to empower memory and concentration while safely revealing patterns of thoughts and feelings.

The Mindful Doodle Book: 75 Creative Exercises to Help You Live in the Moment provides the mental health professional and client with simple, flexible, fun ways to access selected ordinary and extraordinary life experiences.

The doodling exercises invite and inspire active engagement in the present moment, making the invisible, visible. Each chapter touches on heart-felt moments of living. Armed with a pen or pencil and this book, you and your clients can integrate these spontaneous artmaking experiences to promote authenticity, a kind acceptance of yourself, and sense of presence amidst a hectic world.

Doodle Research

Historically, doodling has been viewed as a time-waster and a response to dawdling or daydreaming. However, neuroscientists and other researchers have demonstrated that doodling has many positive side effects. Recent studies indicate that doodling can enhance focusing skills, increase retention of information, ease feelings of impatience, provide ventilation for emotions, and even inspire bursts of insight or novel ideas. The blank page can also serve as an opportunity for revision and elaboration of creative thoughts and ideas. (Roche et al, 2007; Smallwood et al, 2007; Andrade, 2009; Kercood & Banda, 2012; Brown, 2014; Shellenbarger, 2014).

Consequently, doodling is receiving more prestige and status than ever before. Sunni Brown, author of *The Doodle Revolution* (2014), says that it can help us problem-solve and process information. Some research even demonstrates that the brain's default networks may remain active with doodling. These are regions in the cerebral cortex that maintain a baseline of activity when outside stimuli are absent. When we doodle, we do not daydream. Actually, daydreaming takes a lot of cognitive energy as it requires executive functioning unlike doodling (Andrade, 2009). Clearly, doodling helps us focus and maintain concentration during a long meeting or phone call. Additionally, doodling can hasten us to discover solutions as it illuminates different areas of the brain and helps us to analyze information visually. Finally, doodling assists us to deal with challenges as it supports tailoring our focus and improving definition and recognition of the problem at hand.

In her book, Brown focuses most on two studies from the United Kingdom to support her theories. In one, 40 people were told to listen to an extremely boring voicemail going through the names of people attending a party. Half just listened while the other half of the participants were asked to doodle while listening. The doodlers were able to recall 29% more information than the non-doodlers. The study interpreted these findings to mean that "doodling while working can be beneficial."

The other study showed that a group of students asked to draw visuals while reading a science lesson showed a "strikingly" higher ability to engage and clarify the material compared with students who only read and summarized by writing. Brown believes that "there is no such thing as a mindless doodle."

When one doodles, one is uncluttering the mind and a whole lot more. Doodling is both a cognitive act and a calming experience. As Sunni Brown writes, "You can use doodling as a tool. . . to change your physical and neurological experience, in that moment."

HOW TO USE THIS BOOK

The exercises in this book are designed to inspire the mindful doodler through a variety of real life scenarios. Due to the personal and emotional potential of each mindful doodle experience, it is essential for the mental health professional to first try out the doodles for themselves. The personal practice allows for a felt experience at an intimate level, along with an opportunity for self-awareness and validation. One also can build an empathic understanding of the process by participating independently in advance of utilizing these tools with your clients.

Setting, Media Choice, Intention, Doodle Selection

For both the mental health professional and the client, create a safe and comfortable setting free from distraction and disturbance. It is most important to offer an environment that is engaging, inspiring and success-oriented. **Keep the media choices simple, flexible, and limited**. Offer either a pencil, pen or sharpie depending on what is most comforting to the doodler.

A pencil allows for full control and the ability to erase which tends to ease anxiety. Alternatively, a pen, colored pencil or sharpie requires a little more risk and commitment, as the marks are permanent and what one considers a mistake can be incorporated into the doodle design. Any "mistake" is a teachable opportunity for "learning from our mistakes," and the doodle can support this process.

Create an intention (to make the experience meaningful while bringing direction and anchoring in the present moment). For example, you could offer yourself an opportunity to "be present with what is," "cultivate acceptance of my life," or "be kind to myself."

Select a doodle exercise from the Table of Contents that most resonates with you now and read it carefully. Practice as best you can. When ready, allow your hand to move without attachment to the outcome, releasing the mind to doodle spontaneously and intuitively. The time allotment for the whole practice is open to the intention and context for each mindful doodler.

Choosing the Mindful Doodle Exercise for Your Client or Group

Each mindful doodle exercise is an invaluable tool for making selected moments tangible and meaningful with present moment awareness blended with doodling.

The doodle book evolves from *emotions* to *thoughts* to *hopes* to *experiences* to *sensory-based awareness*. Depending on the treatment goals, intention and context, carefully discern what is most present and clinically beneficial for your client(s). For example, the doodle selection can be primarily diagnostic. If your client is suffering from panic attacks due to perfectionism, you may offer the anxiety doodle. To reinforce a cognitive behavioral approach, you might choose the What's On My Mind? doodle exercise. From a positive psychology perspective, consider the Dialogue with The Most Supportive Voice or Resilience Doodle. Be clear about your clinical direction.

If possible, you can certainly offer your client(s) a menu of options and let them choose. That way, there can be a sense of control and resonance with the exercises. Either way, the doodle or series of doodles may provide an opportunity to process issues and highlight strengths with your client(s) or just validate and punctuate a particular perspective and experience.

Selected Doodle Prompts and Doodle Outcomes

In Chapter 1, The Beginning, there is a clear explanation of the difference between a scribble and a doodle.

In Chapter 2, Doodling Feelings (Emotional Landscapes), plain borders individually encapsulate the mindful doodle exercises in order to create safe boundaries for the doodles. Since emotions are deeply personal, there are no doodle prompts in this section.

In Chapters 3, 4, 5, and 6, doodle prompts and borders appear following each exercise. These simple images are designed to inspire and engage the doodler by either building their imagery or doodling in proximity to the prompt. A blank page is also available beneath the exercise and prompt for independent doodling. Whichever approach feels most safe and comfortable is completely up to the doodler.

Art Therapy vs. Therapeutic Art Making for Doodle Processes and Outcomes

While many therapists ask their clients to engage in art making during sessions, many are also left wondering about how to integrate these experiences with clinical fidelity. For mindful doodling, it is essential to know the boundaries of practice with therapeutic art making in order to determine when art therapy is clinically appropriate.

Some mindful doodlers will be satisfied with the doodle experience alone and find the resulting imagery a tool for validation and ventilation of their experience. In this case, therapeutic art making is fitting. When others are invested in looking deeper into their doodles to enhance self-awareness, art therapy may be the most ethical and effective approach.

Art therapy involves a prescriptive utilization of art methods and media, the use of metaphorical and symbolic communication along with psychological theories and approaches in order to assess client status, form appropriate goals, and evaluate responsiveness to treatment by a qualified art therapist. Understanding a client's personal use of materials, processes, symbols, and reflection is crucial to successful treatment outcomes.

Using art therapeutically means to offer success-oriented simple and safe art materials with a few steps and clear directions within your scope of clinical practice. Consultation with or referral to a trained art therapist is invaluable for this work, depending on your goals and the response of your clients to the art experience.

Guidelines for Non-Art Therapists Using Art

These guidelines are partially adapted from:

"Ethical Considerations Regarding The Therapeutic Use of Art By Disciplines Outside The Field Of Art Therapy" (American Art Therapy Association; July, 2000)

- Make yourself an ally in the client's creative process.
- Encourage individual expression and avoid imposing your own views.
- Consider the possible hazards of all materials and equipment being utilized.
- Create a work area that allows messiness and is not hard to clean in order to inspire creativity.
- Be comfortable and familiar with the media and art processes you are using. Art can provoke intense emotional reactions, it is imperative to assess for possible risk factors and prepare for potential outcomes.
- Encourage your client to do what he or she can and offer support as needed.
- Promote individual expression. Avoid imposing your own aesthetic values.
- Be respectful of artwork.

- Consider the imagery to be an extension of your client. Carefully observe your client for any change in affect or behavior before, during, or after the doodle exercise. (If you are unsure what direction to take, consult an art therapist or refer the client to an art therapist.)
- Be mindful of self-conscious or self-critical reactions to the artwork.
- Let the doodle be a visual aide or catalyst for other personal growth work or to develop a leisure skill, or build strengths.
- Ask open-ended questions and encourage the client's impressions.
- Avoid projections, analyses, or interpretations.
- Treat the doodle and its contents as confidential information.

Consultation with or Referral to an Art Therapist

The **American Art Therapy Association** (AATA) recommends that non-art therapists using art should seek consultation or referral with an art therapist if:

- A client demonstrates intense affect/or change during or after an art experience
- A client has a tendency to intellectualize or is emotionally blocked
- A client has experienced pre-verbal trauma
- A client has unresolved trauma or grief or has difficulty making a developmental transition
- A client prefers to express thoughts, feelings, and needs through visual images
- A client's artwork is disturbing to you and you have questions regarding how to respond to it
- The therapist wants information about how to respond to client artwork
- The therapist wants information about the therapeutic use of art

If you find yourself wondering about how to integrate your clients' mindful doodling responses into your understanding and practice of psychotherapy, contact AATA via their website at www.arttherapy.org and find a trained art therapist in your area through the Art Therapist Locator link.

Be mindful of working with untrained professionals who may call themselves art therapists. To achieve the credential of art therapist, one must complete graduate training from an accredited university and receive postgraduate supervision. The profession is quite specialized due to the extensive and rigorous clinical skills needed to safely and competently evaluate and adapt interventions using art media and the creative process.

Case Example: Laura

"Laura" is a young professional female adult suffering from acute anxiety over a historical conflict with her step-parent. Laura independently chose to respond to the mindful anxiety doodle exercise. She eased into the mindfulness meditation practice and completed her doodle in a relatively short period of time. She spontaneously titled it "Loose Ends." Laura went on to speak further about the doodle saying, "As a way to protect myself throughout my life, I have tied things up with a neat bow so I could go on and be cordial in my relationship to my step-parent, despite the relentless verbal and emotional abuse that I encountered. . . However, after all these years, the cumulative effect of the trauma appears to have been unleashed from this uneven book that is coming unbound. Things are pouring out as demonstrated by the doodle and my episodic crying and panic responses to this challenging period." Laura appreciated the parallel process of her interpretation of her doodle and the validation of her current emotional response to the circumstances. She reported feeling "relieved" following the process. Due to the extensive history of abuse and Laura's reliance on her imagery to support her healing process, art therapy would be most beneficial.

Case Example: Denise

"Denise" is a 79-year-old retired widow who was highly motivated to independently choose the Transition Doodle for herself. Denise easily settled into her body following her reading and practicing of the mindfulness exercise. With a pen, she quickly attacked the paper, creating loops on top of each other, which almost looked like a scribble. Denise aggressively pressed into the paper so hard that she tore it in two separate spots. She then wrote the word NO! in four places around the paper. She described her experience as one fighting the transition she is facing with the aging of her body. She spoke irritably about aches and pains along with losing her hair. When asked to look at her doodle and notice the intensity of what she has been carrying in her body, Denise paused and then said, "I actually feel lighter now than I did before I finished this." She then acknowledged that her relationship to that part of herself was shifted, as she could now look at it from a different perspective, and reported feeling greater calmness in the process. Denise was able to regulate her emotions and benefitted from her own experience of releasing her story and stress from aging through mindful doodling. Denise may be a good candidate for using art as a therapeutic tool as she appears to focus more on her affect and story than her imagery.

Disclaimer

Please note that *The Mindful Doodle Book* is not a substitute for medication or other evidenced-based psychotherapeutic approaches. *The Mindful Doodle Book* is a resource for promoting mindfulness practice, self-expression, awareness, and acceptance. The exercises are varied and flexible so that they can be executed independently or with a mental health professional, coach, or art therapist. Alternatively, mindful doodling with this book can easily be a part of a group process. The doodles can serve as both calming devices and catalysts for insight as well as focus points for enhanced concentration and ventilation. No artistic talent or mindfulness meditation experience is required in advance. Practice being with yourself completely as you are in the present, and then doodle it up!

CHAPTER 1
The Beginning

In this introduction, you will experience the distinctive differences between scribbling and doodling. It is important to understand the contrast. Mindful doodling requires present moment awareness without judgment and on purpose. Scribbling is both random and without direction.

The Difference between a Doodle and a Scribble

1. With one color, and your eyes closed, begin to randomly move the pen or pencil around the paper with no agenda. Do not attempt to control the movement. Open your eyes after 15-30 seconds. What do you see in the design?

This is NOT a doodle. Rather, this is a scribble, because it was random and without direction. It is how we all start to communicate and make art when we are between 0-5 years old. Doodling, by contrast, is life long, often organized intentionally, and full of familiar themes and signature imagery. It's truly impossible to make a mistake.

2. Now, choose one color, take a moment and close your eyes and make an intention for your doodle. For example, do you want to have a playful time, release all judgment, accept the process and outcome, relax, ventilate. . .etc.? Keep the intention simple without using the word "want" and creating it for the here and now. Begin anywhere on the paper and allow your hand to move by intuition rather than thought-provoked plans. Go with the flow without trying to make it look a certain way, just allowing the movement and line on the paper for as long as you like.

Notice first how it feels in your body to be without judgment or expectation. See if you can respond rather than react to the image with compassion and kindness.
This IS MINDFUL DOODLING.

To create a mindful doodle:

- Make an intention.
- Release all judgment and expectation of the process and outcome.
- Create with kindness and compassion.
- Take as much or as little time as you wish.
- Cultivate awareness of your body through your senses to promote presence.

CHAPTER 2

Doodling Feelings

EMOTIONAL LANDSCAPES

Emotions run the gamut of unforgettable joys to painful sorrows. They impact our stress reactions and are often in the center of our life experience. Mindfulness invites us to approach our emotions, no matter how challenging, with curiosity and friendliness. It is a moment-to-moment practice that requires great care and refined attention. Intense emotions tend to drive us into automatic reactive mode. Their potency makes it extremely difficult to pause and view them with clarity and objectivity. We tend to become the reaction rather than observing the process. Even less dramatic emotions have many textures and variations and often shift quickly and become hard to notice and explore.

When we choose mindfully to view our emotional life through doodling, we can gently follow our feelings more closely so that we are no longer stuck in a rut of reactivity. Doodling is a playful, soothing task, which can alleviate some of the initial pain felt with intense emotions. It takes time to attend to our emotions with kindness and care, and when we do, we are learning a great deal about ourselves. We allow all our emotions to occur independently without attaching to judgments or thoughts about them. Through the doodle designs, we may notice that in certain situations we find repetitive patterns. With practice, we can explore the reasons for these patterns and how they may be related to events from the past and help us plan for the future. We can actually "feel" and be present for more of our life. **Mindful doodling of emotions can guide us to a greater sense of compassion toward others and ourselves and promote a wide and rich human experience of aliveness.**

When doodling selected emotions, we are giving form to our sensory perception of how that emotion looks and moves in the here and now. Paired with the practice of checking in and noticing our bodies and minds at the moment of experiencing a particular emotion, doodling helps us to remain focused. It creates a safe buffer and a place to view our feeling state with acceptance. The doodle creates a distance between the emotion and our usual behavior around it. Following, the doodle pulls us into the role of kind observer rather than tortured participant. Viewing the outcome of the doodle documents the entire process of the experience of that emotion and how it may have changed, softened, and transformed due to our curious and gentle attention. In mindfully doodling, we choose to make the emotion tangible and familiar rather than remaining abstract and or menacing.

Start with a less intense emotion and catch it right in the moment of its emergence. Notice if it occurs in a particular place in your body. What are the sensations or qualities of it? Come closer to it and begin to doodle what you notice. Watch the doodle reveal the subtle or distinct shifts in the emotion and your response-ability. When you feel ready, begin to address the emotions that are more extreme.

Looking back over your doodles in this chapter will offer you a visual understanding of how you handle various emotions in different settings. You can revisit your doodle whenever you wish, and you will be better able to positively impact your emotions and move toward living a more serene and balanced life.

Happy Doodle

Choose whether you want to document a current happy moment or think back to a happy time and doodle your memory. The intention here is to fully open and allow the experience of happiness to resound whether it is here and now or remembered. Sit in an attentive posture with arms and legs uncrossed. Enjoy the feeling of happiness in your body and mind. Begin to doodle and soak it up!

Sad Doodle

Sit with the feelings and sensations that you know as sadness. Similarly, sad feelings can be reflected upon in the moment or from a memory. Since sad is considered a difficult emotion and is often avoided or ignored, the meditation and accompanying doodle will help you guide your experience with safety and curiosity.

9

Grief Doodle

Grief is a multi-faceted emotion. It is circuitous, that is it runs in a circle, not a line. There is no beginning, middle, or end to it. Grief emerges generally in response to a loss, big or small.

See if you can pause in the wake of this experience of grief. Place a hand over your heart and acknowledge the pain of grief by labeling it and noting where it is living in your body now. You are not trying to make it go away. Rather, you are offering yourself some compassion for this difficult emotional response in your body and in your life now.

Allow your attention to grief to be loving and kind as you would be toward a pet or young child who is in pain.

Take baby steps to hold grief tenderly. Consider saying loving words to yourself such as *"I will be okay"* or *"This is human and natural because of my situation now."*

Doodle what comforts you as you allow grief to be just as it is now.

Fear Doodle

Fear is a scary emotion. The experience is one we often fight or run from instinctively.

See if you can label it and find it in your body now? Fear may be accompanied by other emotions like anger, sadness, resentment, and disappointment to name a few.

See if you can discern fear by itself. If not, that is totally natural. Just taking the time to notice fear is a huge undertaking. This is the practice of turning toward every emotion with kind attention simply because it is part of our experience in this moment.

Practice sitting with fear if you can. If this is overwhelming, then sit with your eyes open and focus on your breathing or another object of attention that you resonate with such as sounds or sensations.

Take baby steps to get to know fear if you feel ready.

Doodle what comforts you as you allow fear to be just as it is now.

Joyful Doodle

We live for uplifting moments of joy. Take this opportunity to pause as you stand firmly in your place of joy. Take in the full essence of your joy inside and out. Doodle it up.

Hatred Doodle

Since hate is such a strong and charged emotion, it tends to provoke dramatic reactions. When the feeling of hate rises up, let it be a teacher rather than an enemy. Breathe with the emotion without trying to change it. Then doodle it exactly as you see it and feel it.

Angry Doodle

Anger is an emotion that is strong and full of energy. As you sit and get close to it with your breath and senses, note if it can transform with your kind and close attention. Doodle the process.

Disappointment Doodle

Sit comfortably with an alert and comfortable posture. See if you can locate the emotion of disappointment in your body. Practice sitting with your experience of disappointment—as if you were greeting the arrival of an uninvited guest with hospitality and curiosity. With your senses, get as close to disappointment as you can. Does it have a shape, color, texture, sound, fragrance, or taste? If it had a voice, would it have something to tell you? Does it have something to teach you? Can you allow it to be just as it is? Doodle your full experience of disappointment in this moment.

Self-Love Doodle

It is difficult for many people to feel love and compassion for themselves. A loving-kindness practice offers us a chance to wish ourselves well. Sit in a straight and noble fashion with your hands on your lap, palms up or down or cupped (whatever is most comfortable). Relax in your body and begin to say to yourself silently, "May I be happy, May I be healthy, May I be free from suffering, and May I live my life with ease." If these wishes do not resonate with your heart, then create your own. Repeat each phrase 3 times saying it with care and meaning. Following this nourishing meditation, doodle your response.

Now you are warmed up for the Loving Others Doodle.

Loving Others Doodle

Sit in the same posture as you did for the Self-Love Doodle and repeat the same phrases. Picture those who you feel love for either individually or within a group. You will say to yourself silently "May you be happy, may you be healthy, may you be free from suffering and may you live your life with ease" (3 times each with care and meaning). Then doodle your response. What does the doodle reveal to you about your loving relationships?

Jealousy Doodle

Jealousy is a complicated emotion. Jealousy often blends with other feelings such as rage, fear, anxiety and humiliation. All of these are unpleasant and we tend to avoid or resist them. Typically, jealousy is part of a thought drama scenario related to feelings of insecurity around a human connection.

See if you can pause in the wake of this experience of jealousy, stand up and ground yourself into this present moment. Breathe deeply and slowly exhale noticing how your body lets go as the breath is released.

In the same way, allow your attention to jealousy to be steady and curious. Label it and find it in your body now. This is the practice of turning toward every emotion with kind attention simply because it is part of our experience in this moment.

Practice taking a stand with jealousy if you can tolerate it. If this is overwhelming, then sit comfortably with your eyes open and focus on your breathing or another object of attention that you resonate with, such as sounds or sensations.

Take baby steps to get to know jealousy as you feel ready.

Doodle what comforts you as you allow jealousy to be just as it is now.

Frustration Doodle

We want to have things our way all the time, don't we? When things do not go our way, we may feel frustration. Through mindfulness practice, we can choose to turn toward this emotion and carefully hold it in our awareness by sitting with it gently. When you have a clear picture of the feeling, doodle it.

Sorrow Doodle

Sorrow is a form of extreme sadness. It typically stems from loss and grief experiences. Sorrow, like all emotions, is universal and a part of the human condition. Once you have identified sorrow in yourself, you have already allowed it, simply by noticing and naming the feeling. If you like, consider lying down and quietly going inside to scan your body for sorrow. When you find it, imagine what it looks like, smells like, sounds like, and feels like. Stretch gently and transition to a position where you can doodle your efforts.

Anxiety Doodle

Anxiety is quite common among children, teens, and adults. To mindfully address this difficult emotional state you can observe and offer support to yourself with hospitable attention. Welcome anxiety because it is already there. You can pause briefly and note its form and position in your body or sit quietly with it. Doodle what emerges in your awareness as a result of your willingness to approach, rather than avoid, your anxiety. Does the doodle help to clarify this feeling state? How do you feel afterward?

Excited and Delighted Doodle

Excited and delighted are emotions that go well together. We love them!

Our bodies are elated, lit up, and filled with exhilaration in the experience of these two extremely pleasurable feelings.

What does your body need to do to express excitement and delight now? Are you jumping up and down, smiling broadly, catching your breath, or just sitting with amazement? Notice your response to this feeling state.

Capture it all in a doodle.

CHAPTER 3
Doodling Mind

THOUGHTS AS EVENTS, MENTAL LANDSCAPE, MEMORIES, IDEAS, DECISION-MAKING AND PROBLEM-SOLVING

Thoughts are occurring in our minds most of the time. When we pause and look at them through mindful doodling, we are able to understand that our thoughts are just events in the mind. Even though we often believe them and live by them, they are frequently inaccurate. The doodle exercises here bring us opportunities to notice our thought patterns and how they impact our lives. The doodles can reveal to us habits of thinking, which then help us clarify decisions and dilemmas, as well as memories and ideas.

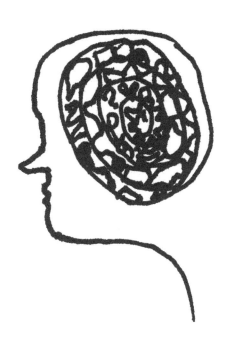

What's On My Mind? Doodle

Check in with your mind. Your thoughts are coming and going like clouds in the sky. Notice the front, center, and back of your mind. Is it open or closed, noisy or quiet, thick or thin? Now that you are paying kind attention to your mind, doodle the contents without judgment or blame. Take note of the placement of your thoughts as they appear within your doodle. What do you see?

Deep Thinking Doodle

Do you consider yourself to be a deep thinker? What does that mean to you? Select a thought that you have given considerable attention to. Notice if it is also loaded with judgment and emotion. See if you can dissect the thought all by itself. Sit and notice how this thought impacts your body, your attitude, your reaction or response. Doodle the process.

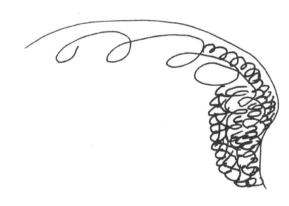

Dense Doodle

In times of crisis or emotional upheaval, our thoughts can be quite overpowering and dense. They can easily cloud our awareness of what is really happening presently. Find a moment to settle yourself, either sitting still or lying down attentively. Be with each breath, each sensation, each thought, and the spaces in between. Thank yourself for taking this time to accept where you are. Now you can doodle it all together.

Doodle Diaries

If you keep a journal already you may want to use the doodles here to inspire further writing regarding your commitment to moment-to-moment presence for fully knowing yourself and your habits of mind.

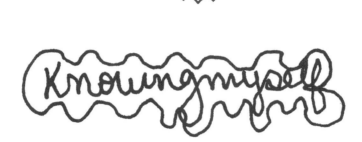

Procrastination Doodle

The pushes and pulls of the thinking mind can easily take over our intentions and behaviors. We often believe what we think and then live our lives according to our beliefs, which can be completely inaccurate. We procrastinate when we think that we want to avoid facing something that we believe and expect to be boring, unpleasant, or painful.

This is another grand opportunity to bring ourselves out of this passive place and actively be with exactly what is going on for us in our bodies and in our lives. Take several deep breaths wherever you are in a quiet place without distractions. Doodle what is.

Playful Doodle

Kids can play often and well. Grown-ups have a harder time because we take ourselves and our thoughts far too seriously. Take some time to stretch your body where ever you feel it calls for a gentle stretch. Make animal sounds with each pose and offer a gesture with your hands and face. Can you be silly? Notice your body and mind. Doodle it up.

Doubtful Doodle

Do you ever think, "Why is this happening to me? Nothing goes my way. I cannot get it right!" Along with this line of thinking there are generally difficult emotions that join in, such as doubt. Allow doubt to come closer to your kind awareness through sitting practice and breath awareness. Now, doodle your doubt. Does the doodle expose a different form and relationship than your original thoughts had you believe?

Dreamy Doodle

Do you remember any of your dreams? Select one that you wish to examine more carefully. Once sitting or lying down in an attentive posture, start with your breath and then include all that you notice inside and outside your body. Allow the dream to come into your mind. With present moment awareness, be completely with all that emerges in your awareness of the dream. When you open your eyes, create your dreamy doodle.

Stress Relief Doodle

We all have stress from many different sources. We naturally try to get away from it or fight it. When you are willing to make time, sit or lie down in your meditation pose and focus on the sensation of breathing, either in your belly or the tip of your nose. With care, redirect your attention back to the breath as many times as it wanders off. Develop an attitude of curiosity and friendliness. When you can, doodle your new attitude and see if your experience of stress is transformed.

Concentration Doodle

Light a candle or focus on one object that is stationary in your surroundings. Sit eye level with this focal point and settle into your body. You are concentrating on one object only. Each time that you notice the wandering mind, tenderly bring it back to the object as many times as you need to.

If you prefer, you can also focus only on your breath, or sounds, inside or outside your body, or sensations throughout your body.

When you feel ready, as you continue to concentrate on your selected object, doodle your experience.

Positive Thinking Doodle

Make an intention for your mindfulness practice in the spirit of cultivating vitality for a positive attitude, positive thoughts, and manifesting friendliness toward yourself here and now.

Sit in a comfortable posture with a relaxed yet straight back and tucked chin. Place your hands gently on your lap or on your heart reminding you that this is an opportunity to give affection to yourself and your life in this moment. Close your eyes.

Smile on the inside as you experience this breath nourishing your whole being as it comes in and out like waves on the ocean. Create an affectionate landscape for the thoughts coming and going in your mind. When you are ready, open your eyes and doodle your response to this exercise.

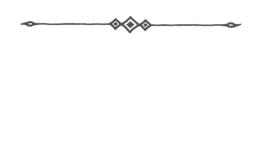

Reflection Doodle

Is there a situation in your life right now that you need to deeply contemplate? See if you can sit in a quiet place, picturing yourself in this situation with all your thoughts, emotions, and judgments around it. Posture yourself in an alert, yet relaxed position.

As thoughts come up, note them as "thinking or thought forms." As feelings come up, note them as "feeling or naming the emotion, such as fear or hurt." If you like, place a gentle hand over your heart or some other comforting place as you consider these current circumstances.

At your pace, take as much time as you need. Then doodle your perspective.

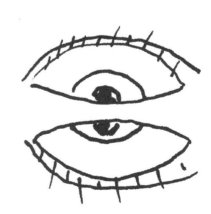

Lost in Thought Doodle

We go through much of our lives with a preoccupation on our thoughts which often pull us out of touch with reality. The mind tends to slant toward negative thoughts due to evolution in the cave days, when we had to be preoccupied with survival which required us to be on guard from the past and the future.

Similarly, the thoughts that snag us into a virtual reality are typically filled with challenging emotions and prophecies. Choose a thought stream that you are entangled with.

Pause and take a few slow, deep breaths, exhaling slowly as you feel your body releasing any tensions.

With an open mind, look at the series of thoughts, emotions, and assumptions that fill your mind.

Doodle what you notice.

Clearing my Mind Doodle

Sit, stand, or lie down with attention to your posture, your comfort level, and your alertness. Focus on your hands or feet only. Take in all that you notice. Is there tingling, heat, coolness, moisture, dryness, tension, or nothing at all? What is going on in your mind now?

Doodle what you notice with all your senses.

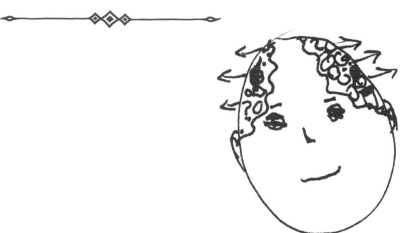

Sentimental Doodle

Nostalgic and tender feelings and thoughts can easily take us over. Sit upright or lie down, maintaining an awake state. Observe yourself as the thoughts and feelings may also have images attached to them.

Allow everything with an open heart, simply because it is happening in this moment. If you suddenly feel pain, place a hand over your heart or another comforting place to offer yourself some compassion.

You are not trying to make the pain go away. You are simply offering yourself some comfort due to the presence of pain. Stay with the whole experience with a gentle and affectionate attitude.

Take as much time as you need. Then doodle your experience, pleasant, unpleasant, or neutral.

CHAPTER 4
Doodling Hopes, Aspirations & Dreams

There are many ways to visualize future goals and desires. Having a clear intention of what we are seeking along with giving kind attention to those wishes allows us to begin to appreciate where we are now and what is actually possible for us. We are often stuck in one view of ourselves and our hopes for what is ahead. Choose which of these mindful doodling exercises will help you most now on your life journey as it unfolds.

Present Moment Awareness Doodle

Mindfulness can slow down the felt sense of time passing. It is possible to linger in the here and now through silent attentiveness without having to have anything happen next and without any purpose other than being alive and appreciative of this life in this very moment. Stop wherever you are and take a breath. Check in with yourself fully on the inside and on the outside. Then, doodle this moment from the inside outward. Feel free to include any turbulence, resistance, and vulnerability as these features frequently undermine our state of presence. Both the mindfulness practice and accompanying doodle can offer us new options for working with the mystery of both the emptiness and the fullness of time passages from moment to moment.

Looking Ahead
1 Year Doodle

Sit in a dignified posture and settle into your awareness of each full inhalation and each full exhalation.

Check in with your whole body, notice any sensations, emotions, and thoughts with a smile. Visualize your path for this year of your one wild and precious life. What do you see, hear, feel, taste and smell?

When you have a clear picture, open your eyes and doodle your one year path.

Looking Ahead 5 Years Doodle

Follow the directions for the looking ahead 1 year doodle, and expand your path to cover 5 years. Notice milestones, open yourself up to all possibilities. Organize your doodle to fit this timeframe.

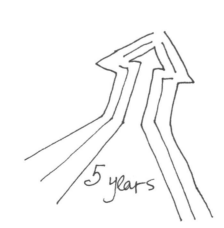

5 years

Looking Ahead 10 Years Doodle

It may be helpful to first experience the 1 and 5 years ahead doodle before attempting this decade doodle exercise.

See what happens in your formal sitting practice as you engage your awareness first with your breath and body awareness and then further allowing your view of the next decade to unfold in your mind's eye. As you gain clarity with the imagery, note the best time to begin to doodle your next ten years.

Honoring Mentors/ Teachers Doodle

Make a list of the most significant teachers or mentors in your life right now. In stillness, stand or sit and visualize one of them in your mind's eye. What qualities does this person have that they have made such a difference in your life? Doodle your connection to this individual and how you have honored them in your own way.

Transitions Doodle

Change occurs in each moment, creating big or little transitions depending on the context and perspective. Our resistance to the inevitability of change and resulting transition can create considerable discomfort. Turning toward these unhappy thoughts, sensations, and emotions brings a freshness and softness to the shift toward the unfamiliar. Sit with yourself, centered, and grounded either on a cushion with legs crossed Indian style or in a straight back chair. Uncross hands and sit with an alert and relaxed posture. Breathe into the experience of unwelcome transition. Note your observations inside. Now, open your eyes and doodle away. Does it look like it felt before you took the time to know it non-judgmentally?

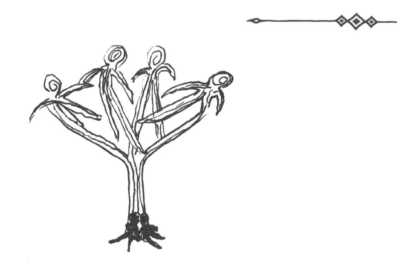

Road Blocks Doodle

Sometimes we think and feel like we are getting nowhere in the pursuit of our hopes and dreams. This kind of absolute belief creates a roadblock for us, and yet it may be a sign of growth after all.

Sit or lie down with an attentive yet comfortable posture. Bring your awareness to your breath and then notice the feelings and thoughts that you are having around being blocked. Get close to them as they come and go inside your body. Notice, allow. When you are ready, open your eyes and see what happens when you doodle this experience. Consider dancing with your doodle. Do you have a different perspective now?

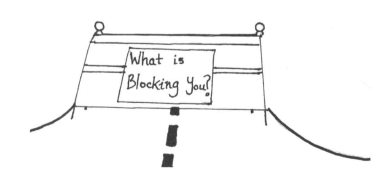

Greatest Achievements Doodle

When you think of your greatest achievement now, what comes up? Is it outside of you or inside?

Being fully in this moment, just as you are, with kind attention is a great achievement. Sit in a dignified yet relaxed posture, join your attention to your breath and celebrate your greatest achievements in your mind's eye. When you feel ready, open your eyes and doodle your response to the experience.

Resilience Doodle

When we are crushed by life's challenges, there is opportunity for growth and renewal. Look back on a situation in your life that felt insurmountable, yet now is resolved.

Sit with the memories, emotions and sensations. Now, connect with your current state inside and outside. See if you notice where you have grown and found strength. Doodle your discoveries.

Doodle Drive

Have you ever driven somewhere and not been sure how you got there? We often drive on automatic pilot with many distractions such as the radio, food, thoughts, talking on the phone, or putting on make-up.

For this exercise, choose to make an effort to be present for as much of your drive as you can. Notice your foot alternatively on the accelerator and brake, your hands on the steering wheel, and take in the full picture of the road. When you arrive at your destination, doodle your experience of this drive. What do you notice? How does the doodle inform your experience?

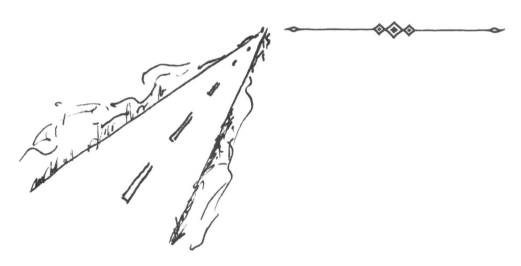

Visions Doodle

Having a personal vision as part of your mindfulness meditation practice is necessary for promoting motivation and continuity. When you doodle your vision you are documenting through your imagery, which you can then display prominently as a reminder of your ideal.

A vision can be composed of what or who you could be if you let go of limiting beliefs, behavior, and habits of thought. Imagine a vision of vitality and excellent health or one of self-compassion and kindness, or of wisdom and generosity. Sit quietly in an attentive posture, close your eyes and notice your breath. Check in with your body and mind. Consider what is most vital to you now. What would it look like for you to be at your best and at peace with yourself as you are?

Take as much or little time as you like and doodle your response to your personal vision. Know that your vision will emerge from what you most desire for yourself. Allow your doodle to mark what you value most deeply.

Priorities Doodle

Looking inside and outside ourselves and becoming aware of the steady stream of judgments and evaluations in which we normally are caught up in cultivates mindfulness. Our minds constantly label and categorize what we believe is valuable to us. We tend to look at things as pleasant, unpleasant, or neutral. Our priorities, or where we put most of our time and attention, spring from these critiques.

The intent of mindful doodling our priorities offers us a judgment-free view of what we value most in our precious lives now. Revisit this exercise from time to time to allow yourself to see the shifts in your choices toward a more balanced life.

Make an intention to discover and explore your current life priorities. Sit in an alert yet relaxed posture for as long as you wish with your hands and feet uncrossed. Notice your breath and then expand your awareness to include your sense of sounds inside and outside your body and the spaces between them. See if you can expand your awareness further to include your sense of touch, feeling your body on the chair or meditation cushion and your feet on the floor. Allow your thoughts to settle on your biggest immediate priority. Notice your body as you explore this area that you are devoting so much attention and time to. Open your eyes and begin to doodle your awareness relying on your senses and breath throughout the process.

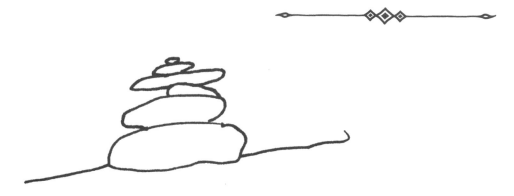

Gratitude Doodle

An attitude of gratitude offers us opportunities to savor what we have in the moment. When you mindfully doodle your gratitude experience, you allow yourself to celebrate thankfulness with form and depth.

The doodle serves both as a reference and reminder of appreciation and, in turn, hope for the future. You can simply make a list of 3-10 things that you appreciate about yourself and or your life. Choose one item that calls forth your attention and sit with it. Notice your breath and expand your awareness to whatever is inside and outside your body at present. Consider what you cherish. What happens to your mood, your emotions, the experience of your body and mind? Now doodle. Continue down your list as you wish.

There is a considerable amount of research that shows gratitude can significantly decrease symptoms of depression and increase positive moods for up to six months! This doodle activity could possibly serve as an anchor for reliving the feelings of appreciation and further enhance the positive results.

Perhaps, simply doodling and viewing the doodle would reinforce this valuable effect.

Digestion Doodle

Mindfulness is about being open and accepting of yourself for who you are. We digest so much from day to day. Whenever we consume, or take in with our senses, we can choose to pause and notice the impact of some of these events with kindness and care. The intention is to first notice our habits of consumption. Do you find yourself around a lot of gossip, spending a great deal of time playing violent video games, or watching the late night news before bed? Our media diet informs our perspectives and preferences.

Begin with one facet of your life that you find yourself having difficulty digesting. As you sit quietly in an attentive posture, gently review the order of steps you follow to take in this habitual pattern of behavior. Doodle each step as you notice them.

Is there a rhythm that you can see? What is the energy like in the doodle? Does the line quality change in certain areas? Take note with a friendly attitude. Are you comforted or disturbed by the doodle? Open and allow your full experience simply because that is your experience now. Deepen your awareness as you bring selected facets of your life outside, inside, and view the effects.

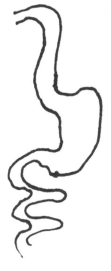

Reality Doodle

Sit comfortably in a posture that promotes wakefulness. Find a place that is relatively quiet and free from distractions. Ask yourself the question, "What is my experience right now?" Look gently at your surroundings and note colors, shapes, shadows, and textures—whatever you take in with your eyes.

Then close your eyes (if you are comfortable doing so) and take in sounds inside and outside with the spaces between them. If you like, place a hand on your chest or belly to remind you of your heartbeat and breathing rhythm and those sounds as well.

Shift your attention (when you are ready) to the feel of your body as a whole as you sit here, with the air around you, your hands on your lap, your feet on the floor.

Then notice any smells around you, pleasant or unpleasant. It may be quite subtle. When you like, gently shift your focus to any flavors or sensations on your tongue.

Allow your entire experience of being alive in this precious moment just as you are. Smile inside and outside bringing a friendly attitude to whatever you encounter in the spirit of what is really going on, rather than what we think is going on or worrying about. . . .
Now, doodle your actual reality.

CHAPTER 5
Doodling Experiences

ORDINARY, EXTRAORDINARY, OR PEAK: HOW DO WE DECIDE TO LABEL EACH EXPERIENCE?

When we ask ourselves what our way is, rather than pushing to get our way, we can understand our habits of how we take in what happens to us from moment to moment. These doodle exercises offer windows to each experience with openness, authenticity, and vitality.

Dark and Light Doodle

To embrace all the joys and wonder of life, we must become fully aware of our aliveness. Attempts to avoid dark emotions serve to actually trap us in them. This exercise is designed to offer you a close, safe, and friendly look at what you consider dark and light inside your body now. In a comfortable position, begin by noticing your breath. Gently scan your body for what you perceive as dark regions and light regions. Take the time you need, then doodle your expression of these experiences.

Doctors Office Doodle

Entering and sitting in a doctor's office can afford us an opportunity to pause in our busy lives. We can choose to notice how we carry ourselves into the office, how we sit and fill the time before we see the doctor. What is happening inside your body? Gently let your breath guide you. Name the emotions that emerge in your awareness, whether they are pleasant, unpleasant, or neutral. Take in the area outside of your body as well. When ready, doodle the entire experience.

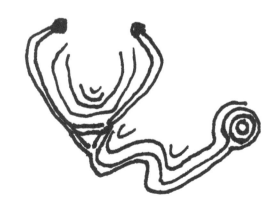

Sports Doodle

Perhaps you were just involved in an experience requiring physical exertion and skill, which might have been competitive and or entertaining. You also may have just chosen to behave in a positive way to respond to a trying situation. In either case, sit, take in your breath and body with affection and ease. Settle into this moment and experience through your doodle. Make it effortless, yet deliberate.

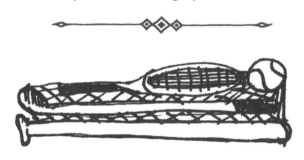

Adventure Doodle

An adventure can be internal or external. Typically, it is an unusual and sometimes risky activity or experience involving the exploration of unfamiliar territory. Find a relaxed position for your body that promotes alert attention and curiosity. Scan your body from the top of your head to the tip of your toes like a kind explorer. Note the temperature of the air around you and any sounds that emerge inside or out. Review the adventure you are currently having in your life. Like it or not, make friends with your experience. What does it have to show you? Doodle with a welcoming attitude and see what happens.

Prayer Doodle

Prayer can be a way of exploring our spirituality and enhancing a dimension that is already part of our busy lives. Anytime we reflect on our relationships, inside and outside our families, and or things we feel grateful for, that is a beautiful prayer. Prayer begins with ourselves and then can expand to include our connection with something greater than ourselves. After you pray, doodle your experience.

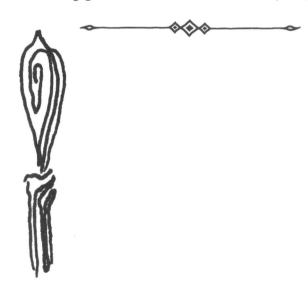

Life Doodle

You can choose to meditate in the midst of some perfectly ordinary life activity. For example, let's say that you are preparing food, or taking out the trash, or doing the dishes. You pause to offer yourself a spontaneous, rich experience making the ordinary life event extraordinary because of the kind of special attention you are giving it. You get a taste of what it is like to be fully with it all as it unfolds. It can then be a magic moment. Grab it. Don't let it slip away. Doodle it.

Traveling Doodle

When traveling, you're already more aware of your surroundings. Meditation will promote mindfulness or kind awareness and acceptance of anything that you are giving attention to during your travels.

Being a passenger on a subway, bus, train, boat, plane or other form of transportation can provide you with the opportunity to meditate as the journey meanders on. Shut your eyes and concentrate only on the rhythm of the engine, wheels, tracks, etc. of the transport method. Expand your awareness of the rhythm to include your breath. Count each breath in and each breath out, from one to ten, then return to one again. If you lose your way or your mind drifts, start again from the beginning. Simply relax into now as you remain alert. When you are ready, doodle your experience of breath and rhythm on your commute or journey.

Crossroads Doodle

There are times in our lives when we find ourselves at a crossroads. It could be amidst several decision options or paths that we are considering. Stand up and feel all four corners of both feet on the floor. You are taking a stand in this one wild and precious moment of your life. Notice your body, any sensations, emotions, and thoughts. Allow everything. If you are comfortable doing so, close your eyes. If not, look at an object in the room that is stationary to promote balance. Picture in your mind's eye, all the possibilities around you. Ask yourself inside for an answer. Doodle it.

Pet Doodle

This is a time for you and your animal friends. See if you can relax together. Listen to your breath and body sensations as you lie next to your pets. If possible, notice your pets' breathing in relationship to your own. Doodle your experience.

Marriage & Partnership Doodle

What does it mean to spend some time just being with your experience of marriage and partnership? Is it about being a loving person to each other? It means that, as you understand the twists and turns of being a couple, you can make deliberate choices to respond to your partner with kindness even in challenging situations. Agree on a time to sit together and pay attention to your feelings right now. Where do you feel these emotions in your body? Identify any negative feelings you have and then recognize that you can choose how to respond rather than react, regardless of what you feel. That may mean you listen more closely, and determine what your partner needs from you right now and meet that need as much as you can. Doodle together your efforts to build and sustain a harmonious bond.

Parenting Doodle

Being or acting as a motherly or fatherly figure is a loving and delicate role. Settle into your body as you know the parameters of your parenting habits with yourself and others. Notice if judgments come up. Is there a critical voice dominating your experience as you sit with yourself in this valuable and challenging role? You may also feel very comfortable and confident. Doodle what happens for you.

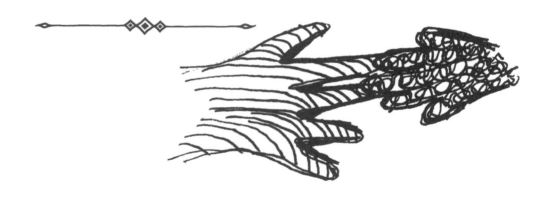

Conflict Resolution Doodle

Mindfulness helps us see that life can be rough for everyone and, at the same time, can shift our relationship to ourselves and others to form deeper connections.

When in conflict, first settle on a time to come together when you are calm. Sit facing each other in a straight, relaxed and alert posture. With your eyes open, notice your breathing and the other's breathing by watching your stomachs. Take at least 1-3 minutes in silence and then gaze into each other's eyes for another 1-3 minutes if possible. Begin to doodle together. Maintain the connection to yourself and the other with presence and intention. Discuss the doodle in relationship to your conflict.

Can you find a resolution in the artwork?

Divorce Doodle

With the decision for divorce, or upon the experience of divorce, take a stand for yourself in your body and your life now. Lift your shoulders up to your ears a few times and then release them. Check in with your breath first. Then, your body. Take three deliberate inhalations and exhale slowly, releasing any tensions or concerns that you no longer need. Then find a place to doodle your experience.

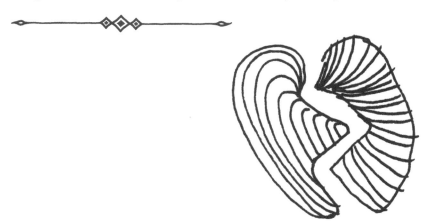

Compassion for Self and Others Doodle

Compassion is the wish that we all be free from suffering. Find a comfortable yet alert posture, whether it is lying down, standing up, or seated upright. Relax your shoulders and uncross arms and legs. Allow the experience of support from either the chair, cushion, mattress, mat/floor, or soles of your feet.

Take three gentle breaths, exhaling slowly and feeling the release of the breath and the impact on your body. Compassion for others softens difficult emotions and challenging life scenarios.

When you are in touch with the part of you that is suffering, whether it is a personal reason or for someone else who is hurting, place your hand on your heart and breathe into that part. Do not try to make it go away. Rather acknowledge the pain with your compassionate attention.

When you feel ready, document the whole experience through doodling.

Death Doodle

Death is something we all have in common. Consider all the losses we encounter in our lives. We often deny death, yet it is the most universal process. Death is quite unpleasant and we like to block its reality out of our presence. This common reaction creates anxiety and disappointment as we are confronted with mortality in many ways. When you are confronted with a loss, take notice and face the moment. Be with your breath, either walking, standing, sitting, or lying down. When you are ready, let your awareness settle on your experience of death. Use your senses. As you open your eyes, doodle your perspective. As you view the doodle, can you find some support for living each day more fully?

CHAPTER 6

Doodling your Universe

SENSORY - BASED AWARENESS

The senses are usually thought of in isolation of one another. However, all of them work together to construct sensory impressions of our world. In this chapter, inspirations for the doodles are drawn from your senses: sight, smell, sound, taste, and touch. The doodles help you to tune into your surroundings, focusing on particular sensations. By deliberately tuning into your senses through doodling, you will gain an increased awareness of your habitual ways of viewing the internal and external world you live in, helping you to consider and document the possibilities in each moment.

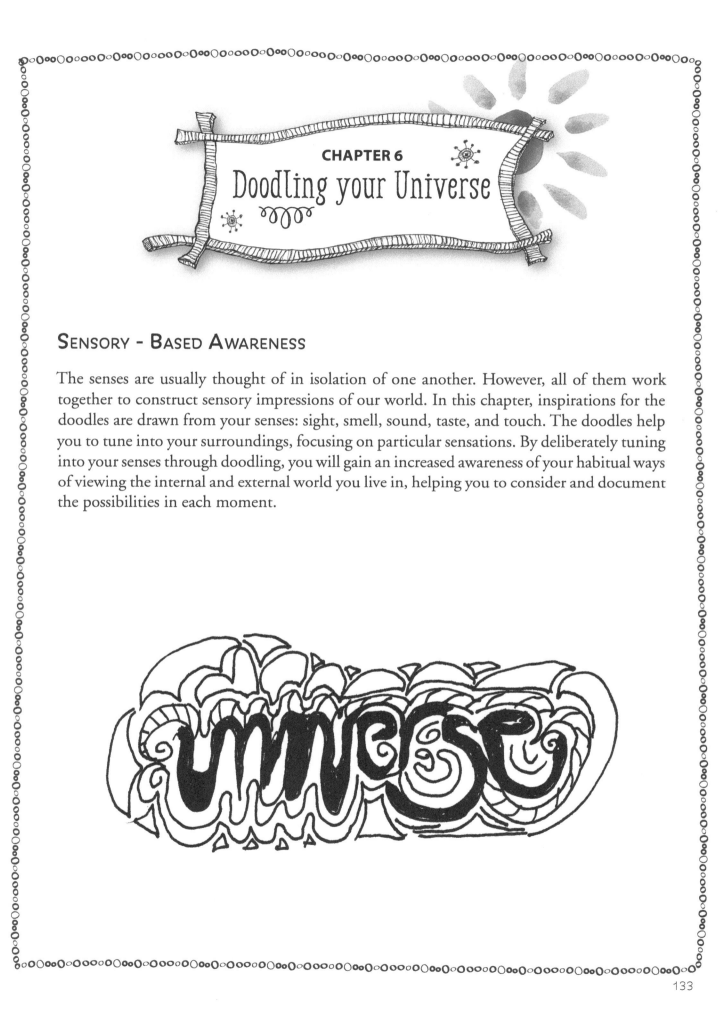

My View of Now Doodle

Take time to find a place where you can be comfortable and without interference by the phone or other people. Sit quietly for 1-3 minutes and notice your breath and body. Take note of any sensations, emotions, thoughts, and judgments that may emerge in your body or thoughts. Look deeply beyond the surface.

Now, begin to doodle your experiences using any lines, shapes, and patterns without trying to form anything in particular. Simply let your doodle appear easily and spontaneously. This offers you a deep appreciation for what is ordinary in your life from moment to moment.

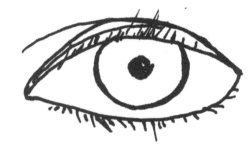

Sounds True Doodle

Find a place to sit inside or outside. Take the time you need to focus on what sounds are present inside and outside your body and the spaces between the sounds. Allow the sounds and spaces you notice to simply emerge in your awareness and then fade away. Then, as you feel ready, doodle your response.

Looking at your "sounds true" doodle, you have documented your authentic experience of hearing now.

How often do we fail to take the time to truly listen to what we hear in our daily lives and note our experience? This doodle concretizes this moment of true listening.

Listening to the Voices Within Doodle

Choose a time when you are alone. Pause for a moment and write down some of the words and phrases that capture your attention with the way you are speaking to yourself through your thoughts at this moment of solitude. Then, doodle around and between them.

View your work with an understanding of the thoughts or loudest voices that you may view as facts habitually. Notice any shapes and patterns without judgment. You might even smile at your doodle and yourself as you begin to recognize these recurring voices and unconscious messages that may inform your behavior.

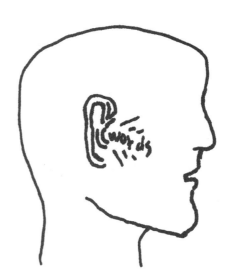

Dialogue with the Inner Critic Doodle

Repeat the directions for the "Listening to the Voices within Doodle," however, only write down the critical remarks you make toward yourself. Notice the difference between this mindful doodling experience and the one before. Compare and contrast the doodle designs. Do they overlap or are they different? Now choose which one feels best to you.

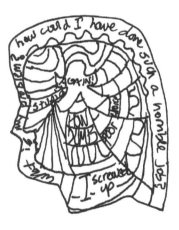

Dialogue with the Most Supportive Voice Doodle

Using the words and phrases from the "inner critic dialogue" doodling experience, begin to doodle from a place of support and guidance. Notice if this changes your experience toward yourself.

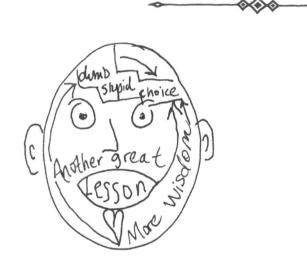

Fragrant Doodle

Pause where you are and notice the smells around you. Are they sweet or fragrant? Make a doodle around your judgment of those fragrances. How does this perspective impact the artwork and your experience of this moment through your sense of smell?

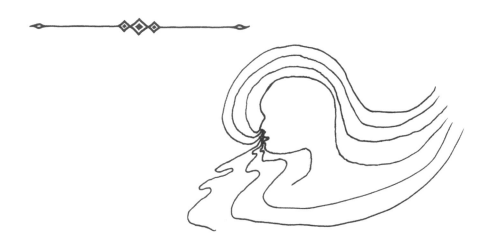

Stinky Doodle

Follow the directions from "Fragrant Doodle," however, notice any scents that you consider to be stinky.

Doodle your experience around that judgment. How does this perspective impact the artwork and your experience of this moment through your sense of smell?

We naturally avoid unpleasant aromas just as we avoid unpleasant feelings and sensations.

Take time to allow your experience and note what happens in the doodle and within your awareness.

The Heat of the Moment Doodle

Step back and take pause when things are too "hot" to handle. This might be because of an argument or situation where you feel overwhelmed or frustrated. See if you can be still and notice where you feel the heat in your body. Let your doodle reveal the actual experience. Do you notice something different that you were not aware of before? Often we jump to conclusions and take things personally.

The mindful doodle exercise gives us a way of ventilating and cooling the flames of the moment.

Tasting Mindfulness Doodle

Select a single bite of a favorite food. Consider how many people were involved in bringing this to you. The sun, rain, soil and farmers helped grow it. It had to be harvested, packaged, and transported to the store. Notice the colors. Put it on your tongue and allow it to change form. Follow it as you chew and swallow. Carefully doodle your experience of taste as the flavors change. Does your tongue hold the memory of this flavor afterward? How does your experience inform your doodle?

Delicious Doodling

After an event that you really enjoyed, doodle your pleasure. Delight in the experience the doodling provides you in both prolonging and remembering this yummy time.

Musical Doodle

Choose a tune in your head or a piece of music that you resonate with. Notice your attitude and emotional state.

Sit in an alert, yet relaxed posture and allow yourself to be with the whole experience of listening to the music, tones, high and low notes, and the spaces between. When you feel ready, either doodle along with the music or following the song. Have you noticed a shift in your attitude or emotions?

Simply open and allow your full experience of the music and your doodle expression of it.

Sticky Doodle

Sometimes it is difficult to let go of things that bother us. They seem to stick with us all day and all night long. We go over the details in our mind repeatedly, trying to find the cause and the solution, motivated to have some control over the outcome . . . and yet, the experience is more like a broken record.

Identify a sticky situation that you are struggling with now. Note the thoughts and emotions stuck within this scenario in your mind. Sit and breathe freely with your eyes closed and imagine yourself watching you from a comfortable distance as you go over the details again and again and again. As a kind observer, drop all judgment and identify each emotion as it emerges along with thinking as the thoughts come and go. After a short time, determine when you are ready to open your eyes and doodle your experience. Does your perspective change when viewing your doodle?

Eye-Catching Doodle

Take a short walk outside and use your senses to savor whatever catches your eye. Notice where your attention goes. What attracts you visually? Take in the colors, scents, textures, movement, sounds, and temperatures. When you are ready, pause, and doodle away.

Gut Feeling/ Intuition Doodle

The gut often helps us make split-second decisions as it delivers cues for us through our body and speaks directly to the mind. Following gut instincts or intuition is often accurate, depending on the situation. Which way is your gut swaying you? Is it heavy, light, crowded, spacious, tense, relaxed, quiet, loud, or a combination of descriptions? Sit with it and digest the whole experience. Pause between breaths and watch for a clearing or a direction. Doodle it up.

Bitter Sweet Doodle

Picture a situation that gives you a mixture of pleasure and pain simultaneously. Open and allow both as each has something to offer you. You may find yourself dominated by the pain and longing for more of the pleasure. This is completely human. See if you can doodle the mix with curiosity and hospitality.

Resources

To contact Dr. Isis, please go to
www.MiamiArtTherapy.com
Check out the link for mindfulness trainings or
Facebook Page: Miami Art Therapy and Mindfulness Trainings

For information on art therapy and locating Registered Board Certified Art Therapists, contact the American Art Therapy Association and The Art Therapy Credentials Board at
www.arttherapy.org and **www.atcb.org**

For information on mindfulness-based approaches, trainings and trained practitioners, contact:
Center for Mindfulness at University of California at San Diego
www.CenterForMSC.org
or
Center for Mindfulness in Medicine, Health Care, and Society
www.umassmed.edu/cfm/

Selected References

American Art Therapy Association (July, 2000). *The Ethical Considerations Regarding The Therapeutic Use of Art By Disciplines Outside the Field of Art Therapy.*

Andrade, J. (2009). What does doodling do? John Wiley & Sons, Ltd. *Appl. Cognit. Psychol.*; 24:100–106.

Brown, S. (2014). The doodle revolution: Unlock the power and think differently. New York: Penguin Group.

Germer, C. (2009). The mindful path to self-compassion. New York: The Guilford Press.

Kabat-Zinn, J. (1990). Full catastrophe living. New York: Bantam Dell.

Kercood, S; Banda, D. R. "The Effects of Added Physical Activity on Performance during a Listening Comprehension Task for Students with and without Attention Problems." *International Journal of Applied Educational Studies* 13:1 (2012): 19–32.

Neff, K. (2011). Self-compassion. New York: HarperCollins.

Roche R.A.P., Commins, S., & Agnew, F., et al. (2007). Concurrent task performance enhances low-level visuomotor learning. *Perception & Psychophysics*, 69, 513–522.

Shellenbarger, S. (July, 2014). The power of the doodle: Improve your focus and memory. *The Wall Street Journal*.

Smallwood, J., Fishman, D. J., & Schooler, J. W. (2007). Counting the cost of an absent mind: Mindwandering as an underrecognized influence on educational performance. *Psychonomic Bulletin & Review*, 14, 230–236.

Smallwood, J., O'Connor, R. C., Sudbery, M. V., & Obonsawin, M. (2007). Mind wandering and dysphoria. *Cognition and Emotion*, 21, 816–842.